WINNING THE VOTE

HISTORY TOPICS

WINNING THE VOTE

SIMON ADAMS

W
FRANKLIN WATTS
LONDON·SYDNEY

ACKNOWLEDGMENTS
The author would like to thank Ann Kramer for her help in
writing the pages on women's suffrage.

Illustrations   David Frankland

Designer   Billin Design Solutions
Editor   Penny Clarke
Art Direction   Jason Anscomb
Editor-in-Chief   John C. Miles

© 2001 Franklin Watts

First published in 2001
by Franklin Watts
96 Leonard Street
London
EC2A 4XD

Franklin Watts Australia
56 O'Riordan Street
Alexandria
NSW 2015

ISBN 0 7496 4248 3

Dewey classification: 324.6

A CIP catalogue record
for this book is available
from the British Library.

Printed in Hong Kong/China

HISTORY TOPICS

CONTENTS

The unreformed House	6
The campaign for reform	8
The parliamentary battle	10
The 1832 Reform Act	12
The Chartists	14
A leap in the dark	16
What about women?	18
Campaigning for change	20
Militant suffragettes	22
Women at war	24
A partial victory	26
Universal suffrage	28
Glossary	30
Index	32

The unreformed House

Today, every man and woman in Britain aged 18 or over can vote in a general election, no matter how rich or poor they are or what part of the country they live in. Two hundred years ago, only a few relatively wealthy men could vote, if they lived in the right place.

> "I was unanimously elected by one elector to represent this ancient borough in Parliament."
>
> Sir Philip Francis, MP for Appleby, Cumbria, 1802

VOTING IN 1800

In the early 1800s only about one in eight male adults could vote. No women had the right to vote. The main qualification was what you owned. You could vote if you owned property or land valued at 40 shillings (£2) or more per year in one of the 84 English, Welsh or Irish counties. In Scottish counties the right to vote was further restricted to those whose property was worth about £100.

These voting rights were established in 1430 in England, in 1542 in Ireland, 1543 in Wales and 1587 in Scotland.

There were five types of borough (town). In scot and lot boroughs every adult male who paid poor rates (to help poor people) could vote. In potwalloper boroughs every adult male resident for more than six months could vote. In burgage boroughs, however, the right to vote was inherited. In corporation boroughs only the members of the town council could vote; and in freeman boroughs only freemen of the town could vote.

MULTIPLE VOTES

There were 658 members of Parliament (MPs) in the House of Commons, and they represented 382 constituencies.

Many constituencies were represented by two or more MPs, and electors each had more than one vote. Each English and Irish county elector had two votes; the two candidates with the most votes won.

By contrast, in the Welsh and Scottish counties each elector had only one vote.

IS THAT A FACT?

ELECTORAL CORRUPTION

Throughout the 18th century elections were very corrupt. Ballots were open to inspection, so everyone could see how an elector voted. Candidates bribed electors, and threatened to punish those who voted the "wrong" way. Elections took place over a couple of weeks to allow remote voters time to vote. They often became very rowdy: drink flowed freely and fights and riots were common.

Many seats were held in the patronage (ownership) of a rich patron. The voters might be his tenants, or could be bribed or threatened to support his preferred candidate. As a result, elections rarely took place in these "pocket boroughs". In Higham Ferrers, Northamptonshire, no election was held between 1702 and 1832, as the seat was controlled by Earl Fitzwilliam.

About half of all MPs had political patrons. Patronage was very expensive, as electors demanded food, drink, travel expenses and other costs to get them to the single polling station in each constituency. Patrons could easily spend £4,000 for each county election and up to £25,000 for a borough election.

Elections in the 1700s could be very rowdy, as depicted by William Hogarth.

FACT FILE

UNEQUAL REPRESENTATION

By 1830 electoral representation bears little relation to where people actually live

- The industrial north of England is badly under-represented: urban Lancashire has 1,337,000 people and 14 MPs, while rural Cornwall has 192,000 people but 44 MPs

- Southern England is over-represented: the six southernmost English counties have one-third of English MPs (162 out of 489) but only one-seventh of its population

- Each English county returns two MPs regardless of its population: Yorkshire has 23,000 voters, Rutland has 800

- All big towns are under-represented: Manchester (182,000), Birmingham (144,000), Leeds (123,000) and Sheffield (92,000) have no MPs at all

- Some towns had almost ceased to exist but still have two MPs: Dunwich, Suffolk, is largely under the sea and has only 32 electors while Old Sarum outside Salisbury has only 11 electors. These constituencies are known as "rotten boroughs"

In 197 boroughs, electors had two votes, but in 63, they only had one; in the City of London and Weymouth, they had four! If a voter was also a graduate or fellow of Oxford or Cambridge University he could vote twice there as well, or once if a graduate of Trinity College, Dublin.

NO CHANGE
The main problem with this system was that it had not changed for centuries. Rising property values meant that voters might be men of great wealth or just owners of small gardens. Changes in population had also played a part in this unfair and unequal representation.

Many small boroughs had two MPs, while some large cities had none. In addition, the huge rise in the population from about 8 million in 1700 to 24 million in 1830 was not reflected in an increased number of electors, which had risen from 240,000 to only 440,000 in the same period.

The campaign for reform

During the second half of the 18th century, pressure for parliamentary reform increased. But reformers were divided among themselves. After the French Revolution broke out in 1789 many turned against reform as they feared that any change might lead to revolution in Britain.

> "The remedy consists ... of a reform of the Commons ... as shall give every payer of direct taxes a vote at elections."
>
> William Cobbett, *Political Register*, 1816

WHAT TYPE OF REFORM?

There were three main causes behind the rise of the reform movement. The first was the widespread objection to patronage and corruption in Parliament, particularly in the government of Lord North (1770-82), which kept itself in power through control of the rotten boroughs despite losing the American colonies during the War of Independence. The second was the unfairness of representation as industrial cities grew in size and wealth but remained unrepresented, while small boroughs continued to have an unfairly large number of MPs.

The third was the most important. Across Europe, Enlightenment thinkers discussed the best form of government. The French philosopher Jean-Jacques Rousseau's book, *The Social Contract* (1762), was particularly influential.

In it he argued that a contract existed between governors and governed which rested on the right of the governed to choose their political masters in a democratic fashion. These ideas of democracy were very strong in Britain and were taken up by many reformers, notably Tom Paine.

Reformers were, however, divided among themselves. Some just wanted to eliminate the worst features of the system without losing any of their own power. Others wanted a far more democratic system which would allow most if not all adult citizens to vote in elections. None of them wanted to give women the vote, as they did not consider them to be full citizens.

REFORM OR REVOLUTION?

Until the French Revolution, the reform movement in Britain was led largely by those in Parliament who wanted to reform the system from within.

PAINE

Tom Paine (1737-1809) was the son of a Norfolk farmer. He worked as an excise officer, but was sacked for demanding higher pay. When the French Revolution broke out in 1789, Paine supported the revolutionaries. In 1791-92 he published *The Rights of Man*, which argued in favour of universal manhood suffrage and radical social reform. The book influenced many people.

In 1819 troops broke up a reform meeting in Manchester, causing many deaths.

The work of the reformers continued after the French Revolution broke out, but they were joined by groups of radicals outside Parliament who wanted far wider reforms. These groups included the Yorkshire Association, set up in 1779, and the London Corresponding Society, which was formed in 1792.

However, the upheavals of the French Revolution convinced many reformers that reform would quickly lead to revolution. Prime Minister William Pitt, an early advocate of reform, suppressed all radical activity during the 1790s and used police and troops to break up meetings of the London Corresponding Society.

The cause of reform was revived after Napoleon's defeat in 1815, but the government continued to repress all radical activity. In 1819 11 people died and 400 were wounded when a mass meeting in St Peter's Fields, Manchester was broken up. Pressure for reform increased, but Parliament ignored it.

FACT FILE

PARLIAMENTARY FAILURE

From 1783 to 1830, a series of bills in favour of reform are debated

1785 Prime Minister William Pitt introduces a bill to redistribute 72 rotten borough seats to the counties; it is defeated by 248 votes to 174

1793 A reform proposal by Charles (later Earl) Grey MP is defeated by 282 to 41

1809 Bribery Act prevents MPs bribing their constituents to vote for them; the Act is rarely enforced

1809 Proposal to give all householders the vote massively defeated

1817, 1818 Further reform proposals heavily defeated

1822 Lord John Russell proposes transferring seats from 100 smaller boroughs to larger towns and counties; defeated by 269 votes to 164

1823, 1824, 1826, 1830 Further reform proposals by Russell rejected, as are proposals from a Tory MP in 1829-30

1829 Catholic Emancipation Act allows Roman Catholics to sit as MPs

The parliamentary battle

In November 1830 the Tory government of the Duke of Wellington resigned. A new Whig government led by Earl Grey took power determined to introduce parliamentary reform. It was the first Whig government for 47 years.

> "The country possesses at the present moment a legislature which answers all the good purposes of legislation."
>
> Duke of Wellington in the House of Lords, 2 November 1830

PRESSURE BUILDS

Outside Parliament, pressure for reform was growing. In 1830 a rich banker, Thomas Attwood, formed a "General Political Union between the Lower and the Middle classes of the people" in Birmingham. Other cities set up their own organizations, holding demonstrations and rallies and sending numerous petitions to Parliament demanding reform. As the law then required, a general election was held after George IV's death.

The election was held in July-August 1830 and as a result a large number of MPs who opposed reform lost their seats.

The Tory government had been in power since 1783, but by November 1830 it was falling apart. Some Tories, like the Duke of Wellington, were strongly against all reform, while a more liberal group wanted limited change. When Wellington came out clearly against reform on 2 November 1830 these liberal Tories shifted their support to the opposition party of Earl Grey. Wellington resigned two weeks later, and Grey became the new Prime Minister.

FIGHTING FOR REFORM

The First Reform Bill was introduced into the House of Commons in March 1831 by Lord John Russell, as Earl Grey sat in the House of Lords. It was far more radical than most MPs expected and within a month the government was defeated on an amendment (proposed change) to the bill and resigned. New elections returned a huge majority for reform. Russell introduced a Second Reform Bill in June, which was agreed by the Commons in September.

GREY

Charles Grey (1764-1845) was a life-long campaigner for parliamentary reform. He became a Whig MP in 1786 and introduced his first reform bill in 1793. He tried again in 1797, but despaired of any reform as long as the Tory Party ruled the country. In 1807 he became an earl and went to the House of Lords. Although he had served briefly as First Lord of the Admiralty and then Foreign Secretary in 1806-07, he remained in opposition until he became Prime Minister in 1830. As Prime Minister, he fought to get the Reform Act through Parliament.

This cartoon shows King William IV wondering if the Reform message is for him.

For a bill to become law, it has to be agreed by both Houses of Parliament. The Commons wanted reform, but the Lords — unaffected by the bill, which only dealt with elections to the Commons — disagreed. In October 1831 they rejected the second bill. Riots immediately erupted across the country; many people feared that revolution would break out if the bill was not agreed.

Grey therefore introduced a Third Reform Bill in December 1831. In order to break the deadlock, he asked the king to create enough pro-reform Whig peers to get the bill passed. William IV agreed to this extraordinary proposal, but when the bill was defeated in the House of Lords in May, he refused to create 50 to 60 new peers immediately. Grey resigned.

Wellington, however, could not form a new government, so William IV asked Grey to return and agreed to create enough new peers to pass the bill.

The Lords gave in: on 4 June 106 voted in favour and 22 against — most did not vote. The Third Reform Bill received the royal assent and became law. Similar bills for Scotland and Ireland became law soon after.

FACT FILE

BATTLE FOR REFORM

March 1831 First Reform Bill introduced into House of Commons

April 1831 Government defeated; Parliament dissolved

April-May 1831 Whigs win general election and introduce Second Reform Bill in June

September 1831 Second Reform Bill is agreed by House of Commons by 345 to 236 votes

October 1831 House of Lords rejects Second Reform Bill

December 1831 Third Reform Bill introduced

January 1832 William IV agrees to create enough peers to get Reform Bill through

March 1832 Third Reform Bill passed in Commons by 355 to 239

May 1832 House of Lords agrees a hostile amendment. Grey resigns, but Wellington unable to form new government. King again confirms that he will create new peers to force the bill through

June 1832 Third Reform Bill is finally passed by the House of Lords

July 1832 Scottish Reform Bill is passed

August 1832 Irish Reform Bill is passed

The 1832 Reform Act

The House of Commons before it was destroyed by fire in 1834. Nothing had changed for centuries.

The battle for parliamentary reform lasted 18 months from start to finish, with a general election and the involvement of the king necessary to get the bill into law. But what did it include, and how radical was it?

WHAT THE ACT INCLUDED

The main effect of the Reform Act was to redistribute 143 seats from the English boroughs to the English counties and the new industrial towns of the north. Old Sarum, Dunwich and 54 other pocket and rotten boroughs disappeared.

"The final solution of a great constitutional question."
Lord John Russell, 1832

In addition, 30 boroughs with less than 4,000 inhabitants lost one MP each, while Weymouth lost two of its four MPs. In their place, 17 major industrial cities, including Birmingham, Leeds, Manchester and Sheffield, and five London boroughs each gained two MPs, while 21 smaller industrial towns, such as Bury, Gateshead, Rochdale and Wakefield gained their first MP.

12

RUSSELL

Lord John Russell (1792-1878) was first elected a Whig MP in 1813 and remained in the House of Commons until he became an earl in 1861. He supported the reform of Parliament and introduced a series of bills while in opposition between 1822–30. As Paymaster-General he steered the three Reform Bills through the House of Commons in 1831-32. In later years he held other offices of state.

The English and Welsh counties gained 65 seats, Ireland and Scotland a total of 13 seats between them. The complex system of voting qualification was simplified in both borough and county, but here the effect was not very great.

The electorate rose from about 440,000 to 652,000 voters, or from about 1 in 8 adult males to 1 in 5. In Scotland, the number remained at about 1 in 8, while in Ireland, only about 1 in 20 adult men could vote. Women were still not allowed to vote.

THE EFFECTS OF THE ACT
The main idea behind the Reform Act was to get rid of the most objectionable features of the old system and bring the middle classes — property owners, professional people, businessmen and traders — into politics. It introduced moderate reform, not democracy. Earl Grey told the House of Lords in 1831 that he hoped "to prevent the necessity for revolution ... there is no one more dedicated against annual parliaments, universal suffrage and the [secret] ballot than I am."

He succeeded; in 1848, when the rest of Europe erupted in revolution, Britain was relatively unaffected.

The Act was not intended to affect who governed Britain. More members of the middle class entered Parliament, but government was still run by the aristocracy.

The Act did not introduce fairer representation. Small boroughs like Reigate and Westbury, with less than 200 voters, kept their MP, while Croydon, Doncaster and Loughborough, with populations of over 10,000, had none. The English counties gained seats, but had only 32% of MPs to represent 57% of the electorate. Some 70 MPs still represented pocket boroughs.

Grey and Russell saw the Act as a one-off measure, to prevent further reform. Instead, the Act opened the door for more far-reaching reforms.

FACT FILE

THE REFORM ACT

The Reform Act of 1832 both alters the composition of the House of Commons and increases the number of electors

• 87 English boroughs lose one or both of their MPs; 143 seats now available for redistribution

• 22 large English towns each gain two MPs; 21 smaller English and Welsh towns gain one MP each

• Scotland gains eight MPs, Ireland gains five

• English and Welsh counties gain 65 MPs

• Constituencies increase from 382 to 401

• All the borough franchises are replaced by the qualification of owning or occupying property worth at least £10 for over a year

• In English and Welsh counties, freehold land and property owners worth more than £2 per year, £10 copyholders (a type of freeholder) and £50 leaseholders and tenants get the vote

• A proper register of electors is to be compiled in each constituency

The Chartists

Between the passing of the Reform Act in 1832 and the renewed campaigns inside Parliament for further reform in the 1860s, the main group to push for political changes were the Chartists.

> "This Convention is of the opinion that a wanton, flagrant and unjust outrage has been made upon the people by a bloodthirsty and unconstitutional force from London."
>
> Resolution from William Lovett to the Chartist national convention, July 1839

THREE PETITIONS

The Reform Act of 1832 did not end public agitation for parliamentary reform, because almost all working people were still excluded from voting or sitting in Parliament. Associations of working men began to press for change: the London Working Men's Association was set up in 1836, the Birmingham Political Union in 1837 and the Great Northern Union in Leeds in 1838.

In 1839 these and other groups came together in the national Convention of the Industrious Classes.

The Chartist campaign focused on the People's Charter, published in London in May 1838. The idea of a charter was to spell out in a single document the demands of the movement; the name recalled Magna Carta, which had listed the liberties of England in 1215.

The Charter made six demands: universal suffrage for every man (but not woman) aged 21 and over, secret ballots in all elections, the abolition of property qualification for MPs, payment of MPs, equal-sized constituencies, and annual parliaments. A massive petition demanding that Parliament implement the charter was launched in Birmingham at the same time. In June 1839 the first Chartist petition, containing 1,280,000 signatures, was presented to Parliament, which refused by 235 votes to 46 even to discuss it. A second massive petition was again refused by Parliament in May 1842.

Both petitions were accompanied by mass demonstrations, public meetings, riots and attempts to organize a general strike.

REVOLUTION IN EUROPE

In 1848 much of Europe erupted in revolution and governments were overthrown in France and elsewhere. The Chartists saw this as an opportunity to draw up a third petition. They collected 5,706,000 signatures and held a huge demonstration on Kennington Common in South London on 10 April before marching on Parliament to present it. Parliament was frightened and received the petition, but it soon discovered that it contained many spoof signatures, including Queen Victoria and the Duke of Wellington, who had been brought out of retirement to organize the defence of London against a possible Chartist uprising. As a result, the petition was ridiculed and rejected by Parliament.

14

The Chartists held a huge demonstration on Kennington Common in London.

As the economy prospered during the early 1850s, many working people grew richer and withdrew their support from the Chartists. Chartism rapidly declined and the movement came to an end in 1858.

WHY DID CHARTISM FAIL?
Chartism was the first important working-class protest movement in Britain's political history. But it won few middle-class supporters in Parliament. Most MPs felt threatened by its mass appeal and violent activities and thought that Chartism threatened the state. The movement itself was split, between those who wanted to win with the moral force of argument and propaganda and those who argued that only physical force would win their objectives.

However, Chartism did play a crucial role in improving the political self-confidence of working people and later helped them organize in trade unions and other groups. During its lifetime, the six demands of the Charter were never met, but today they form the basis of our democracy, with only the demand for annual parliaments still unmet.

FACT FILE

THE PEOPLE'S CHARTER – THE SIX DEMANDS

1) "A vote for every man twenty one years of age, of sound mind, and not undergoing punishment for crime." – Granted in 1918

2) "The Ballot. To protect the elector in the exercise of his vote." – Secret ballots introduced in 1872

3) "No property qualification for members of Parliament – thus enabling the constituencies to return the man of their choice, be he rich or poor." – Removed in 1858

4) "Payment of members, thus enabling an honest tradesman . . . or other person, to serve a constituency." – MPs first paid in 1911

5) "Equal constituencies, securing the same amount of representation for the same number of electors, instead of allowing small constituencies to swamp the votes of larger ones." – 1948, when business and university votes were abolished

6) "Annual parliaments, thus preventing the most effectual check to bribery and intimidation." – Seven-year parliaments reduced to five years in 1911

A leap in the dark

During the 1860s the two main political parties took up the cause of parliamentary reform. The result was a massive extension of the right to vote within 20 years.

> "Everything is now new and changed and large and I fear I must say in some respects dark."
>
> Lord Glyn, Liberal chief whip, 1868

THE 1867-68 REFORM ACTS

Although most politicians hoped that the 1832 Reform Act had ended the need for further reform, pressure from the Chartists and the continuing growth of industrial towns and cities meant that pressure for change built up in the 1850s. Lord John Russell, who had steered the 1832 Act through Parliament, introduced four new reform bills between 1849-60, while the Conservative Earl of Derby introduced his own bill in 1859. None of them succeeded, because although there was now agreement for reform, no one could decide what form it should take.

The deadlock was broken in 1866. Russell introduced another reform bill as prime minister, but it was defeated by members of his own Liberal party and he resigned. The Conservatives then took power and Disraeli, leader of the party in the Commons, seized the opportunity to introduce his own bill in 1867, thereby splitting the Liberals. A Scottish bill became law in 1868.

The 1867-68 Reform Acts doubled the number of electors from 1.1 to 2 million and gave the vote to richer members of the working class. One-third of all adult males could now vote, although women still could not. As in 1832, seats were redistributed from small boroughs to the industrial towns and the more populated counties.

1884-85 ACTS

One problem with the 1867 Act was that it retained separate franchises in borough and county seats. In 1884 Gladstone, the Liberal prime minister, made them the same. The next year he introduced a massive Redistribution Bill, which created constituencies of roughly equal electorate and size. This came close to the Chartists' demand for "equal constituencies". Again, smaller boroughs lost seats to larger industrial towns, London and under-represented Scotland, Ireland and Wales. The total electorate now numbered 5.6 million, about 3 in 5 of all adult males.

FURTHER REFORMS

During this period several acts of parliament did much to stop electoral corruption. The Corrupt Practices Prevention Act of 1854 levied fines for bribery and intimidation, and made candidates produce accounts of their election expenditure. The Corrupt and Illegal Practices Act of 1883 set limits on election expenditure and introduced severe penalties, including prison, for electoral corruption. In 1858 the property qualification to become an MP was abolished, while the Ballot Act of 1872 introduced secret ballots.

GLADSTONE AND DISRAELI

The two dominant figures in British politics in the later 19th century were the Conservative Benjamin Disraeli (1804-81; right) and the Liberal William Gladstone (1809-98; left).

Disraeli was Prime Minister in 1868 and again in 1874-80. Gladstone was Prime Minister four times between 1868-94. Both tried to make their political parties appeal to the mass of new, working-class electors through social reform, although neither wanted full adult suffrage. The two were bitter enemies: Disraeli thought Gladstone high-minded and pompous, while Gladstone thought Disraeli frivolous and immoral.

These had been two of the Chartists' demands. In 1863 neutral returning officers were appointed to oversee elections, while the Parliamentary Elections Act of 1868 moved control of disputed elections from MPs to the High Court.

IS THAT A FACT?

In 1885, the Redistribution Act moved towards the principle of one-member, equal-sized constituencies. It created 72 new constituencies in the English cities and suburbs. Constituencies were now increasingly defined by class: working-class inner cities, middle-class suburbs and boroughs and landed-class counties.

FACT FILE

1867-68 REFORM ACTS
- 46 small boroughs lose 52 MPs
- 11 new boroughs get 13 MPs
- Birmingham, Leeds, Liverpool, Manchester, Glasgow and Dundee gain three MPs each
- Salford and Merthyr Tydfil both get a second MP
- 11 English counties get two more seats each; Lancashire and Scottish counties three more
- London and Scottish universities get three MPs
- In the boroughs, all householders paying rates and lodgers paying at least £10 a year get the vote
- In the counties, owners of property worth £12 a year or land worth £5 a year can now vote

1884 REFORM ACT
- County franchise becomes the same as 1867 borough franchise
- Those who own land or buildings worth £10 per year get the vote

1885 REDISTRIBUTION ACT
- Small boroughs lose 159 seats
- London gains 40 MPs
- English boroughs gain 32 MPs
- English and Welsh counties gain 66 MPs
- Scotland gains 14 MPs and Ireland 25
- House of Commons increases from 652 to 670 MPs

 What about women?

Today, women have much the same rights as men. Two hundred years ago, however, women had few rights. They had a long, hard struggle to achieve even small changes in the law.

> "I do not wish them [women] to have power over men, but over themselves."
>
> Mary Wollstonecraft, *A Vindication of the Rights of Woman*, 1792

SLOW PROGRESS

At the start of the 19th century, women's legal and social status were inferior to men's. Women were considered to be the weaker sex. They could not vote, or stand for election. By law, a woman was the property of her father first, then her husband. A single woman could own property, but it passed to her husband when she married. A woman could not obtain a divorce, even against a violent husband.

Women did not even have legal rights over their children. Only a few women had access to education, and there were no university places for them. A woman's place, for middle-class women at least, was supposed to be in the home, caring for her husband and children. It was not considered respectable for them to work. Unpaid charitable work was acceptable. Poorer, working-class women did work, combined with their domestic chores. They were paid far less than men, and their work had much lower status.

Women began to challenge this. One was the radical thinker Mary Wollstonecraft, who said that if women had the same intellect as men, they should have equal rights. In the 19th century the law was slowly changed to give married women more rights, particularly over property and legal access to their children. Women could also vote in local elections and stand as councillors. Universities and medical schools were opened to women. The Education Act of 1870 gave girls up to 13 free state education.

WOLLSTONECRAFT

Mary Wollstonecraft (1759-97) was a radical thinker and author. Her formal education was limited, but she taught herself and opened a school for girls in Newington Green, London. In 1787 she wrote of her concerns about the lack of education for women in *Thoughts on the Education of Daughters*.

In 1792, she wrote her most famous book, *A Vindication of the Rights of Woman*. She deliberately took the title from Tom Paine's *Rights of Man*, published in 1791-92, to point out that even a radical thinker like Paine was only concerned with universal male suffrage – that is, votes for all adult men – not universal adult suffrage. Wollstonecraft's strong views on the equality of women were influential in the 19th century, as British women fought to get the vote and other rights.

A women's reform meeting of the 1880s.

By 1900, most towns had a girls' secondary school, and many women had trained as nurses and teachers.

THE RIGHT TO VOTE
However, women could still not vote in national elections, or stand for Parliament. Increasingly, women came to feel that getting the vote would improve their position. They began to form suffrage societies and organize petitions. However, because they could not attend Parliament, they had to rely on sympathetic male MPs to present their case. In 1832, during the debate over the Reform Bill, Henry Hunt MP presented the first petition to Parliament asking for women's suffrage. Parliament refused to discuss it. In 1867, during debates on the second Reform Bill, philosopher John Stuart Mill MP presented another petition and, unsuccessfully, tried to change the bill in favour of women's suffrage. He argued the case more fully in his book *The Subjection of Women* published in 1869.

FACT FILE

WOMEN'S RIGHTS

1839 Custody of Infants Act gives some mothers access to their children in event of separation or divorce

1857 Matrimonial Clauses Act makes divorce easier but grants women fewer rights than men

1869 Municipal Franchise Act allows single women to vote in borough elections

1870 Education Act allows women to vote for and serve on new school boards and provides free elementary education for girls

1870, 1872, 1884 Married Women's Property Acts allow women to keep their own earnings after marriage, to keep property acquired before marriage separate from that of their husbands and to no longer be "chattels" (possessions) of their husbands, but independent persons

1888, 1894 Local Government Acts allow women to vote for new county councils and to vote and stand for urban and district councils

1907 Qualification of Women Act allows women to stand as councillors at county and borough levels

Campaigning for change

Women grew increasingly frustrated at Parliament's failure to grant them the vote. They set up campaigning organizations to advance their cause.

> "The smouldering resentment in women's hearts burst into a flame of revolt. There began one of the strangest battles in all our English history."
>
> Hannah Mitchell, a working-class suffragette, writing about the WSPU in 1905

THE SUFFRAGISTS

The first such groups were set up in northern England in the first half of the 19th century, but they were all short-lived. In 1867, after the defeat of John Stuart Mill's woman's suffrage amendment to the Reform Bill, two new groups were formed in protest. These were the Manchester National Society for Women's Suffrage and the London National Society for Women's Suffrage, founded by Millicent Fawcett and others.

Similar organizations were formed in Bristol, Birmingham and Edinburgh. In 1872 a Central Committee for Women's Suffrage was formed to coordinate all these groups.

By 1897 most major towns and cities had a women's suffrage organization. Some groups overlapped, so 20 groups in London and other cities joined to form the National Union of Women's Suffrage Societies (NUWSS) with Millicent Garrett Fawcett as president.

Its members and supporters were known as suffragists: they consisted mainly of well-educated middle-class women, although a group of radical working-class women in the Lancashire cotton mills also made a great impact working through trade unions and the newly formed Labour Party.

The NUWSS was immensely successful as an organization: by 1913 it had a weekly journal, *The Common Cause*, more than 400 societies across the country, a membership of 500,000 and an annual income of £45,000. It campaigned peacefully through a mixture of public meetings, processions, petitions, letter writing and lobbying. However, despite its size and high public profile, it failed to obtain any change in the law.

FAWCETT

Millicent Garrett (1847-1929) was born in Aldeburgh, Suffolk, and married the Liberal MP Henry Fawcett in 1867. She campaigned for many women's causes, notably full property rights for married women, and devoted her life to women's suffrage. In 1897 she became president of the NUWSS. Millicent Fawcett was opposed to militancy but understood the frustration that caused it.

THE SUFFRAGETTES

Some women felt that the peaceful, non-violent approach of the NUWSS was failing to achieve any success. In 1903 therefore, a new type of radical campaigning organization was set up: the Women's Social and Political Union (WSPU). Founded in Manchester by Emmeline Pankhurst and her daughter Christabel, the WSPU was dedicated to obtaining votes for women "by any means necessary". It soon moved its headquarters to London where, from 1907, it published the weekly paper *Votes for Women*.

The WSPU was never as big as the NUWSS — in 1910 it only had 36,000 members — but was far more militant, and prepared to use direct action to achieve its objective. In 1906 the *Daily Mail* called this group "suffragettes" to distinguish them from the moderate suffragists of the NUWSS.

Suffragette Christabel Pankhurst, as seen by the Vanity Fair cartoonist "Spy" in 1906.

FACT FILE

GETTING THE VOTE

Around the world, women find getting the vote is a slow process

1869 In Wyoming, USA, women get the vote, the first women in the world to gain this right

1881 Women on the Isle of Man vote for the House of Keys (lower house of parliament)

1893 New Zealand is first country to grant women the vote

1908 Limited suffrage in Norway; full suffrage in 1913

1908 Women can vote in all Australian states; they had gained the right to vote in federal elections in 1902

1915 Women gain vote in Denmark and Iceland

1917 Netherlands; Canada: several Canadian provinces had already given women the vote. Women could first stand for Canadian federal elections in 1920

1918 Propertied women over 30 gain the vote in Britain

1920 Women get the vote in the USA

1928 Men and women 21 and over gain the vote in Britain

1945 French women get the vote

Militant suffragettes

Between 1905-14, the suffragettes waged one of the most imaginative and daring campaigns in British political history. Many women suffered great hardship; for all of them, it was a cause they passionately believed in.

> "We are here to claim our right as women, not only to be free, but to fight for freedom. That is our right as well as our duty."
> Christabel Pankhurst, 1911

A NEW TYPE OF POLITICS

In the run-up to the general election in January 1906 the WSPU adopted militant tactics: disrupting election rallies by shouting slogans like "Votes for women" and "Deeds not words". They demanded that candidates should state whether or not they supported women's suffrage. Christabel Pankhurst and Annie Kenney heckled the Liberal candidates Winston Churchill and Sir Edward Grey in Manchester.

The Liberal Party won by a huge majority. Many Liberal MPs supported women's suffrage, but their leadership did not. The WSPU continued their campaign, heckling ministers and staging rallies and marches on Parliament. These were stopped by the police and the marchers arrested. In 1908 a demonstration in Hyde Park, London, was attended by 250,000 people. Some women chained themselves to the iron railings outside the House of Commons.

Many suffragettes were sent to prison. Once there they went on hunger strike. At first they were released, but soon the authorities began to force-feed them. In 1913, after a huge public outcry against this barbarous treatment, the government introduced the Prisoners' Temporary Discharge for Ill-Health Act. Known as the "Cat and Mouse Act", it allowed hunger-strikers to be released when they became ill or weak from lack of food, and then re-arrested when they had recovered enough to finish their sentences.

THE BATTLE INTENSIFIES

In 1910 the Liberal government called two general elections. The first was to get the radical budget it proposed through the House of Lords and the second was to reduce the powers of the Lords.

An all-party group of MPs introduced two Conciliation Bills in an attempt to break the deadlock between the government and the campaigners. The government meanwhile introduced a Reform Bill with the promise of a vote on women's suffrage. In response, the WSPU called off its militant campaign, but in January 1913 the Reform Bill was ruled out of order by the Speaker of the House of Commons.

THE CAMPAIGN BEGINS AGAIN

The WSPU immediately restarted its campaign. Shop windows were broken across London, paintings were slashed in the National Gallery, the home of David Lloyd George (the Chancellor) was set on fire, as were the homes of other politicians, and telegraph wires were cut to disrupt communications.

On Derby Day, 4 June 1913, Emily Davison was trampled as she ran in front of King George V's horse.

The race was disrupted, but Emily Davison suffered massive injuries and later died.

Her funeral turned into a huge demonstration in support of women's suffrage.

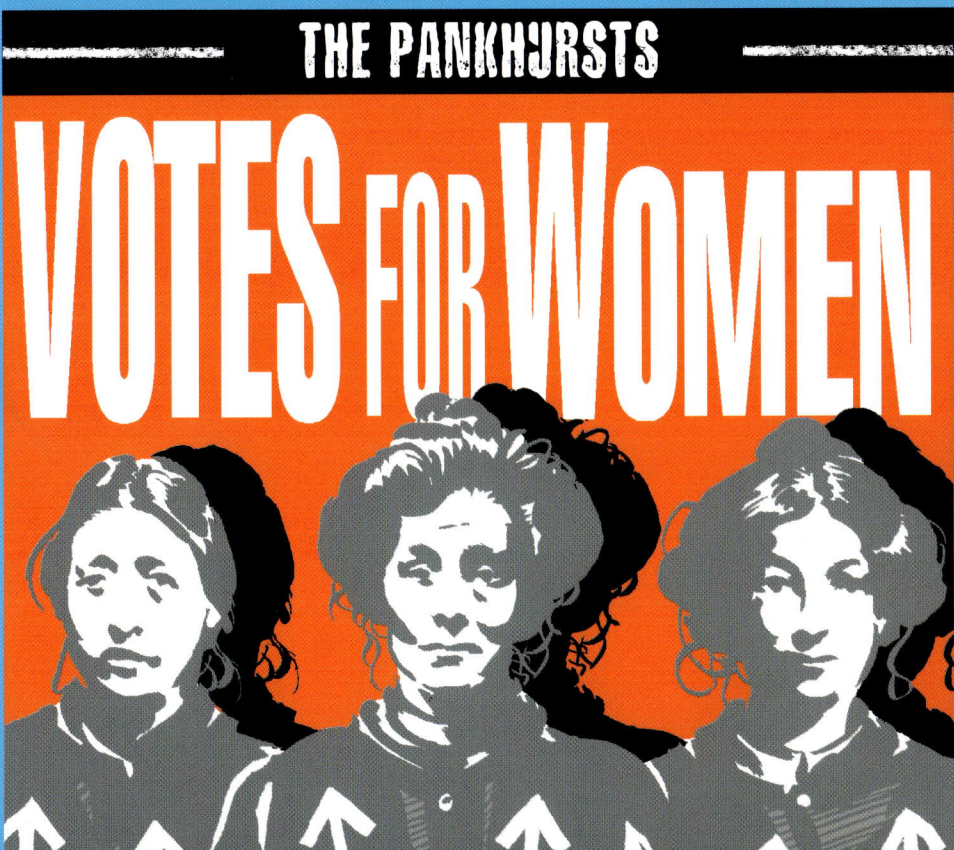

THE PANKHURSTS

VOTES FOR WOMEN

EMMELINE PANKHURST (1858-1928; centre) married the lawyer Richard Pankhurst; they had three daughters and two sons. In 1903 she formed the WSPU with daughter Christabel; later she stood for election as a Conservative candidate. Emmeline, Christabel and Sylvia all endured imprisonment for their cause.

CHRISTABEL PANKHURST (1880-1958; right) co-founded the WSPU with her mother. A brilliant speaker and organizer, she was responsible for planning WSPU strategy. She emigrated to California in 1939.

SYLVIA PANKHURST (1882-1960; left) was also a suffragette, and the WSPU's official artist. She wrote an account of the WSPU in *The Suffragette Movement*. A socialist and pacifist, she championed the cause of Abyssinia (now Ethiopia) against the Italian invasion of 1935-36 and died in its capital, Addis Ababa.

FACT FILE

THE SUFFRAGETTE CAMPAIGN

1903 WSPU is formed in Manchester

1905 WSPU becomes militant; Christabel Pankhurst and Annie Kenney arrested and imprisoned

1906 *Daily Mail* first calls campaigners "suffragettes"

1906 WSPU moves HQ to London

1909 First hunger strikers force-fed in Winson Green prison, Birmingham

1910 Liberals win general election; all-party Conciliation Committee of 54 MPs promotes a Suffrage Bill; WSPU calls a truce

1910 Conciliation Bill is defeated; march on House of Commons ends in police brutality: 150 women are arrested, 50 are seriously injured and two later die

1911 Truce is resumed as second Conciliation Bill gains big majority

1912 Manhood Suffrage Bill introduced; MPs can amend it to include women's suffrage

1913 Manhood Suffrage Bill ruled out of order by Speaker; militant action restarts

1913 "Cat and Mouse Act" introduced

1913 Emily Davison dies

Women at war

In August 1914 Britain declared war on Germany at the outbreak of World War I. Women were divided about the rights and wrongs of the war, but it also gave them their greatest opportunity to win the vote.

> "Women demand the right to serve"
>
> Banner held during suffragette march, London, 17 July 1915

DIVIDED SUFFRAGETTES

As soon as war broke out, the moderate suffragists of the NUWSS expressed their support for the war and ended their non-violent campaign. "Let us prove ourselves worthy of citizenship, whether our claim be recognized or not," wrote Millicent Fawcett, president of the NUWSS, advising her members to suspend political agitation for the vote and concentrate on war work. She hoped that such work would prove women were worthy of the right to vote.

The militant suffragettes of the WSPU, however, were divided. Christabel and Emmeline Pankhurst believed that it was a woman's patriotic duty to support the war. They encouraged all women to get jobs in industry and the armed services in order to free men for military service. Sylvia Pankhurst was a pacifist, however, and disagreed. The WSPU split, and the suffragette campaign ended for the duration of the war.

WAR WORK

Before the war most working-class women worked in factories, mills, sweatshops or in domestic service — all menial jobs. These jobs were also low paid. In fact women were paid less than men and few had any managerial responsibilities. Wealthier, better educated women worked as teachers or nurses or in clerical and secretarial work, although many had to leave their jobs if they got married. For both groups, however, only a few jobs were considered suitable for women; the vast majority were restricted to men alone.

THE WOMEN OF PERVYSE

For some women, the war was a big adventure. Mairi Chisholm was 18 when war broke out. She left her aristocratic family in Scotland and became a despatch rider for the Women's Emergency Corps and then went to Belgium with a nurse, Elsie Knocker, as part of the Flying Ambulance Corps.

In November 1914 the two set up a first-aid post at Pervyse, north of Ypres, and dressed the wounded until both were gassed in early 1918. The two became known as the Women of Pervyse. They were almost the only women on the front line. After the war, the pair were awarded the Belgian Order of Leopold and the British Military Medal.

Women work in a Manchester munitions factory during World War 1.

The war gave women an opportunity to improve both their status and their income. Many left domestic service or low-paid industrial work for better paid, more responsible, and often more exciting, work. This included working in munitions factories, driving ambulances and trams, or in support roles for the fighting services. In these roles they mended engines, drove trucks and did vital administrative work. As more and more men were conscripted (forced by law) into the armed services, women had an increasingly important role in keeping industry, agriculture and essential public services running: about 800,000 women entered industry. Their work on the home front was as important as the role of the troops on the front line, for without them the country would have ground to a halt and the army run out of essential munitions and other equipment. Through their war effort, women gained a freedom and responsibility they had never enjoyed before.

FACT FILE

WOMEN IN WARTIME

August 1914 Women's Emergency Corps, Women's Volunteer Reserve, the Flying Ambulance Corps set up to enlist women into support roles for the army

August 1914 Central Committee on Women's Employment co-ordinates use of women to replace men in regular employment

February 1915 Women's Police Service formed

March 1915 Government compiles register of women willing to do agricultural, industrial and clerical work

April 1915 Glasgow Corporation employs first women tram conductors

May 1915 Manchester suffragists establish Women's War Interests Committee to oversee women's conditions in munitions factories

July 1915 Women's Right to Serve march in London led by Emmeline and Christabel Pankhurst

November 1915 Crèches set up in factories

February 1917 Women's Land Army set up

March 1917 Women's Army Auxiliary Corps formed

April 1918 Women's Royal Air Force formed

A partial victory

In the general election of 1918 women aged 30 and over voted for the first time in their lives. The Votes for Women campaign was over, but how did women achieve this victory, and what sort of victory was it?

THE END OF THE WAR
The general election due in 1915 was postponed until the end of the war. However, when it was held, it was likely that almost all servicemen who had fought for their country would be unable to vote as they had not been resident at their home address for more than one year, as required by the 1884 Reform Act. In addition, some soldiers did not have the right to vote at all. A new reform bill would therefore be needed to allow all men the right to vote.

The prospect of a new bill raised the issue of whether women should finally get the vote. Millicent Fawcett of the NUWSS kept up the pressure on the government and told the Prime Minister, Herbert Asquith, that the suffragists' campaign would restart regardless of the war if the vote was given to all men but not to women. Asquith therefore asked the Speaker of the House of Commons to convene a conference to decide the issue on cross-party lines.

In February 1917 the Speaker's Conference recommended that all men aged 21 and over should get the vote. However, it agreed that only women aged 35 or over who were ratepayers or wives of ratepayers should be able to vote. The government then introduced the Representation of the People Bill in June 1917. During the debate, it introduced a new clause lowering women's suffrage to 30. This was accepted by 385 to 55 votes and went through the House of Lords in January 1918 with a majority of 134 to 71. Further legislation allowed women to stand as candidates for election.

FIRST-TIME VOTERS
As soon as the war ended on 11 November 1918, a general election was called for 14 December. Supporters of women candidates organized mock ballots to show women how to cast their votes and provided childcare facilities so mothers could vote. Christabel Pankhurst and other former suffragettes stood for election, as did some suffragists, 17 women in all. The political parties were not sure how the female electors would vote, although both Liberals and Conservatives feared they would mostly support the Labour Party. In fact they voted in much the same way as men: according to their class, family background, religion or other particular interest.

> "To live to see the triumph of a 'lost' cause for which we have suffered much and would have suffered everything, must be almost the greatest of delights."
>
> **Evelyn Sharp, suffragette**

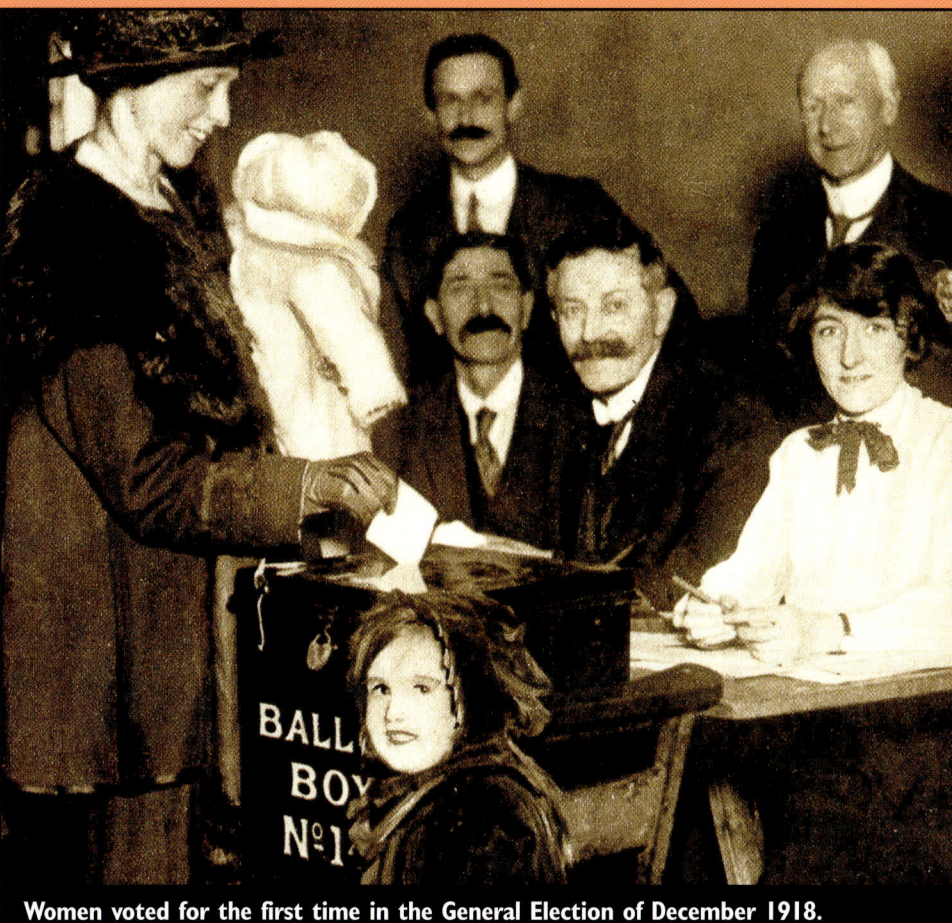

Women voted for the first time in the General Election of December 1918.

FACT FILE

REPRESENTATION OF THE PEOPLE ACT 1918

• All men aged 21 and over get the vote

• All women aged 30 and over who are ratepayers or wives of ratepayers get the vote

• Electorate rises from 7.7 million in 1910 to 21.8 million in 1918 out of a total adult population of 27.4 million

• All 14 million adult men now get the vote, but only about seven million or 55% of adult women

• Number of seats in House of Commons rises from 670 to 707; it drops to 615 in 1922 when Ireland gains its independence from Britain

• For the first time, all voting takes place on a single day

• Parliamentary candidates pay a deposit of £150, which is returned if they get one-eighth of the total vote

• 17 women candidates stand for election, but only one is elected

• Of the unsuccessful candidates, Christabel Pankhurst gets 8,614 votes in Smethwick and narrowly misses winning the seat

THE FIRST WOMEN MPS

Countess Constance Markievicz (1868-1927) was an Irish revolutionary who married a Polish count. Condemned to death for her part in the 1916 Easter Rising in Dublin, her sentence was commuted. In the 1918 general election she was elected Sinn Féin MP for Dublin South. Sinn Féin did not recognize British rule over Ireland so she never sat in the House of Commons.

Nancy Astor (1879-1964), an American, married Waldorf Astor, Conservative MP for Plymouth Sutton. He inherited his father's viscountcy in 1919 and went to the House of Lords. Nancy Astor fought and won his seat in a by-election. She was the only woman in the Commons until 1921 and remained an MP until 1945.

Universal suffrage

Although the Representation of the People Act of 1918 gave some women the vote, women still had fewer rights than men. The campaign for universal adult suffrage was not yet over.

> "The appointment of the first woman cabinet member … has been received today with a general quiet approval."
> *Time and Tide,* June 1929

UNIVERSAL ADULT SUFFRAGE

The campaign to get women the vote in the 1918 Act had been led by the NUWSS; the suffragettes of the WSPU had played no part in the campaign and disbanded before the general election. In 1919 the NUWSS changed its name to the National Union of Societies for Equal Citizenship (NUSEC) and began to campaign on issues wider than the vote, such as equal pay for women and men and the right of teachers to retain their jobs if they got married.

During the 1920s, the campaign to achieve full voting equality continued, but the sight of women voting in elections or sitting in Parliament and, by 1929, the cabinet, was no longer controversial. Likewise, the appointment of the first women solicitors and barristers, or the sight of women driving cars or smoking in public, no longer attracted much attention.

In 1928 the Conservative government of Stanley Baldwin decided to remove the inequality of the 1918 Act and give everyone aged 21 and over the right to vote in both national and local elections regardless of gender or status as ratepayers. Baldwin judged that young women were no more likely to vote Labour than another group in society. Universal adult suffrage had finally arrived, and at the 1929 general election – almost 100 years since the first parliamentary reform act – every adult in Britain could vote.

UNFINISHED BUSINESS

There were a few loose ends that still had to be tied up. In 1948 the Labour government of Clement Attlee finally got rid of plural voting.

New-look Labour in 1997.

This meant that some voters had voted both where they lived and also where they worked or went to university. It also abolished the last 12 two-member seats. A permanent commission was set up to ensure that constituency boundaries reflected population changes.

The Representation of the People Act 1969 reduced the voting age from 21 to 18. An act in 1985 raised candidates' deposits from £150 to £500 to deter "joke" candidates. It gave British citizens resident overseas for five years (20 years from 1989) the right to vote in parliamentary elections. From 1979 voters could vote for the European Parliament's MPs. Since 1999 electors in Scotland and Wales have also voted for their own parliaments.

WILKINSON

Ellen Wilkinson (1891-1947) was a life-long socialist and trade unionist. From 1915-24 she was the national women's organizer for the Union of Shop Distributive and Allied Workers (USDAW). She was a member of the Independent Labour Party and the Communist Party before joining the Labour Party in 1924. Elected MP for Middlesbrough in 1924 – one of only four women MPs elected – she then became MP for the shipbuilding town of Jarrow from 1935-47. In 1936 she led 200 unemployed workers on the famous Jarrow Crusade to London to seek aid for their impoverished town.

WOMEN IN PARLIAMENT

1918	Countess Markievicz is elected first woman MP, but does not take her seat
1919	Lady Astor becomes first woman MP
1922	Two women win seats in general election out of a total of 615
1923	8 women MPs elected; only 4 returned in 1924 election
1929	14 women MPs elected
1929	Labour MP Margaret Bondfield becomes first woman to sit in cabinet, as Minister of Labour
1935	9 women MPs elected
1945	24 women MPs elected
1975	Conservative MP Margaret Thatcher becomes first woman to lead a major British political party
1979	Margaret Thatcher becomes first woman Prime Minister; only one other woman serves in her cabinet during her 11 years as PM
1979	Number of women MPs drops to post-war low of 19 out of 635
1987	41 women MPs elected
1992	60 women MPs elected
1992	Betty Boothroyd becomes first woman Speaker of the House of Commons
1997	121 women win seats out of a total of 659; 101 of them represent the Labour Party

Glossary

ballot — The act of voting by an elector using a ballot paper placed in a ballot box.

Bill — A proposed new law that is debated by Parliament. When it is agreed by both the House of Commons and House of Lords and has received the royal assent it becomes an Act of Parliament.

borough — A town with a royal charter and its own elected council; known as a burgh in Scotland.

candidate — A person standing for election.

constituency — A town or county represented by an MP.

county — A largely rural administrative division (area) of Britain.

democracy — Government by the people or their elected representatives in Parliament.

election — The selection by ballot of a person to represent people in Parliament or elsewhere.

electors — People eligible to vote in an election.

The Enlightenment — Intellectual, political and scientific ideas common in 18th-century Europe which stressed human reason over superstition; also known as the Age of Reason.

freehold — Property or land owned for life, on which no rent is paid; copyhold is a more restricted form of freehold.

general election — Election held when Parliament is dissolved and every MP faces re-election.

MP — A member of Parliament.

Parliament — In Britain, Parliament consists of two houses: the elected House of Commons, where MPs sit, and the unelected House of Lords.

patronage	Control over an MP or a constituency by a rich patron, such as a local landowner.
petition	A written document signed by a large number of people demanding action from the government.
pocket borough	A borough that was held in the "pocket" of a rich patron.
polling station	The place where electors cast their votes.
rotten borough	A borough in which the electorate had largely died out but still had its own MPs.
seat	The parliamentary constituency held by an MP is known as a seat because an MP sits in the House of Commons.
secret ballot	Voting so that no one but you knows how you have cast your vote.
suffrage	The right to vote: universal manhood suffrage is the right of every man to vote, universal adult suffrage the right of every adult (men and women) to vote.
Suffragette	Militant campaigner for women's suffrage; a supporter of the Women's Social and Political Union (WSPU).
Suffragist	Moderate campaigner for women's suffrage; a supporter of the National Union of Women's Suffrage Societies (NUWSS).
Tory	Political party at first opposed to parliamentary reform; during the 1830s it became the Conservative Party.
Whig	Political party in favour of moderate parliamentary reform; during the 1860s it became the Liberal Party, predecessors of the modern Liberal Democrats.

INDEX

A
Asquith, Herbert 22, 26

B
Baldwin, Stanley 28
ballot 6
  Act 16
  secret 13, 15, 16
Birmingham 7, 10, 12, 14, 17, 20, 23
  Political Union 14
boroughs 6, 7, 8, 9, 11, 12, 13, 16, 17
  pocket 6, 12, 13
  rotten 7, 8, 9, 12

C
Central Committee for Women's Suffrage 20
Chartists/Chartism 14-15, 16, 17
cities, industrial 7, 8, 10, 11, 16, 20
Commons, House of 6, 10, 11, 13, 17, 22, 23, 26, 27, 29
Conservatives 16, 17, 23, 26, 27, 28, 29
constituencies 6, 9, 13, 15, 16, 29
Convention of the Industrious Classes 14
Corrupt Practices Prevention Act 1854 16
Corrupt and Illegal Practices Act 1883 16
counties 6, 9
  representation of 7, 9, 11, 13, 16, 17

D
Davison, Emily 23
democracy 8, 13, 15
Disraeli, Benjamin 16, 17

E
Education Act 1870 18
elections, 18th-century 6
electorate, increases in 7, 13, 16, 27
England 6, 7, 12, 13, 14, 17

F
Fawcett, Millicent 20, 24, 26
French Revolution 8, 9

G
Gladstone, William 16, 17
Grey, Charles (later Earl) 9, 10, 11, 13

I
Ireland 6, 7, 11, 13, 16, 17, 27

K
Kenney, Annie 22, 23

L
Labour Party 20, 26, 28, 29
Liberals 16, 17, 22, 23, 26
London 7, 12, 14, 15, 16, 17, 21, 22, 23, 25, 29
  Corresponding Society 9
  National Society for Women's Suffrage 20
  Working Men's Association 14
Lords, House of 10, 11, 12, 22, 26

M
Manchester 7, 9, 11, 12, 17, 22, 23, 25
  National Society for Women's Suffrage 20
Mill, John Stuart 19, 20

N
National Union of Societies for Equal Citizenship (NUSEC) 28
National Union of Women's Suffrage Societies (NUWSS) 20, 21, 24, 26, 28

P
Paine, Tom 8, 18
Pankhurst
  Christabel 21, 22, 23, 24, 25, 26, 27
  Emmeline 21, 23, 24, 25
  Sylvia 23, 24
Parliamentary Elections Act 1868 17
Property, Married Women's Acts 19

R
Reform Acts
  1832 12-13, 14, 16
  1867-68 16, 17
  1884-85 16, 17, 26
reform bills 9, 10, 11, 13, 16, 19, 20, 22, 26
Representation of the People Acts 26, 27, 28, 29
Russell, Lord John 9, 10, 13, 16

S
Scotland 6, 11, 13, 16, 17, 24
suffragettes 21, 22-23, 24, 26, 28
suffragists 20, 21, 24, 25, 26

T
Tories 9, 10
towns 9, 12, 16, 20; *see also* boroughs
trade unions 15, 20, 29

V
votes, number per elector 6, 7, 29
votes, university 7, 15, 17, 29
voting qualifications 6, 13, 15, 16, 17, 19, 26, 27

W
Wales 6, 13, 16, 17
Wellington, Duke of 10, 11, 14
Whigs 10, 11, 13
Wollstonecraft, Mary 18
women
  education of 18, 19
  MPs 27, 29
  property rights 18, 19, 20, 21
  votes for 6, 8, 13, 16, 18-25, 26, 27, 28, 29
Women's Social and Political Union (WSPU) 21, 22, 23, 24, 28
World War I 24-25, 26

PICTURE CREDITS
Tracey Brett: 7, 12, 21
Kieran Doherty/Popperfoto: 28
Mary Evans Picture Library: 9, 11, 15, 19, 25, 27

Whilst every attempt has been made to clear copyright should there be any inadvertent omission please apply in the first instance to the publisher regarding rectification.